Jeff Bowick & Dwayne Henriksen

OPTIONS TRADING CRASH COURSE: FUNDAMENTALS

Everything you need to know before you start investing like a real trader

Table of Contents

INTRODUCTION

In order to master the tools necessary to operate in the financial market and, in particular, to profit from options trading, it is necessary to know well the world in which you are going to operate and the tools you have at your disposal.

Let's start with the main concept: what is online trading?

Online trading is the buying and selling of financial instruments through the web in order to make profits. It is basically buying and selling financial instruments such as CFDs, futures, currencies, bonds, commodities, and other instruments through a trading platform.

A trading platform is a virtual environment where orders can be placed in the market. The platform can be web-based (in which case it is accessed from the browser), or software/app-based (in which case it must be installed before accessing it).

Online trading is very fashionable today. Many practice it and many make profits without having studied for years. This is the beauty of the modern digitized society, which allows you to find the information you need to practice an activity almost everywhere, even trading.

To get headlong into investing, however, you need to know what you are doing, and that is the purpose of this handbook: to provide you with the preliminary tools that will allow you to better understand the vast amount of information that can be found on the web and, perhaps, to help you make a selection between what is useful and what is not.

Our aim is not to discourage you from trading, far from it. We just want you to feel that you are ready.

Because online trading has many advantages and, if done correctly, it can really change your life.

It is an activity that can be done from the comfort of your home, from your office, your computer, your smartphone or your tablet. All you need is access to a secure, regulated trading platform and an internet connection. That's it.

Online trading operates in a short time: in fact, once you have bought a security you can sell it again in no time.

The costs are reduced, as the commission costs are generally quite low.

Regulated investment platforms, among other things, offer precise and detailed information on the trend of any security, with the possibility of viewing charts, to have information on a financial instrument and markets in general, etc.. All this allows the trader to make investment choices with greater awareness.

Another benefit of online trading, especially if you use trading platforms, is the ability to devote even a few minutes a day to trading or to exploit the potential of automatic trading by setting orders, stop losses and target profits through the trading platform. This practice - automatic trading - optimizes your operations, automating them and avoids losing good profits and running into big losses in case of sudden market declines, if you were not physically in front of the computer at an uncertain moment. The system will work for you according to your instructions and you will be at peace. Not bad, right?

Finally, with trading platforms you will have a wide range of financial instruments at your disposal to be able to invest your money according to your most disparate needs (more or less risk, more or less capital, more or less return etc.).

Let's not forget, however, that online trading is an activity that also has disadvantages such as the riskiness and costs associated with trading (overnight commissions, spreads etc.).

This is why we recommend that you read this manual carefully and make all the information contained in it your own. That way you will be really ready to face the world out there!

CHAPTER 1   BEFORE STARTING

When you trade options you don't have to buy or sell shares. Instead you buy or sell options. Options are time based contracts that give the owners the right to buy or sell shares in a company at a particular price within a certain timeframe.

This means that options are simple but powerful tools. They can help you to make a profit at any time and in any market. But they must be used correctly.

You should know about these six important things in order to get a good start with option trading.

1. How to trade options; how to read an option; what the price of an option is telling you, and how the price of an option works

2. Understanding how the options market works, related to options and the price of an option: how option prices are calculated; what early exercise dates mean; why calls are more expensive than puts

3. The six pieces of information you have to know about options trading: what they are; how you have to read them, and how to use them.

4. How to make a plan for your trading career, including an understanding of the different types of trades and when you should use them.

5. The seven types of strategies and how to choose the right one for you

6. How to know when you should get out of your position

You are needed to have a thought of what by and large options exchange is. Mull over the different wordings utilized in this field. This may incorporate terms, for example, a holder, an author, a striking spot. And so forth, it is fitting to think of an accounting page with these phrasings and put forth an attempt to contemplate them inside and out. This will contribute a ton to your comprehension of what Option Trade spins around. By and large, options exchange can be characterized as an agreement that permits you to one or the other purchase or sell a stock at a specific strike price for a predetermined timeframe. With this information, you have just begun making your means towards Option Trading. You understand that options trading generally spins around the call option just as the put option and subsequently the need to guarantee that you comprehend what they involve inside and out. The options as a rule assume a basic part; they control the value of the stock. You ought to likewise comprehend that the options are inclined to terminate, particularly in situations where the agreement is finished.

For this situation, you wind up losing your expenses to the designer.

While continuing with how to begin Options Trading, you will need to have united the essential apparatuses. This alludes to different assets that will be sufficiently adequate to take you through the whole cycle of Option Trade.

Your capital assumes an extremely basic part in guaranteeing that you can buy an option that best suits your methodology and be in a situation to amerce however many benefits as would be prudent. In the situations where you plan on including a representative, you can easily provide food for their payments just as be in a situation to employ their best administrations.

The other advance that you should acclimate yourself with is the information and understanding that options exchange includes high dangers. The dangers here are as a rule in two measurements, the measure of money you lose when contrasted with the benefits you would have understood, the other measurement is the likelihood of obtaining benefits when contrasted with the likelihood of getting a misfortune. The high dangers can happen, particularly when the options have been bought theoretically. In the event that at one point you are not cautious, you may wind up losing every one of your benefits. You can without much of a stretch gain high benefits in the event that you have an inside and out comprehension of the stock's price development. Exploiting the options in such situations can disappear up into ensuring your speculations past a sensible uncertainty. For this situation, you just remain to lose the charges and a tiny level of the speculation, as you had portrayed in the agreement.

Getting to the most basic parts now, you should open a money market fund either on the web or customarily through a representative. Here there are different variables to consider prior to settling with the most dependable financier organization.

Guarantee that you know about their expenses and motivators. A portion of the business organizations might be offering limits to their clients to draw in them, and you can exploit this and advantage from the limits they offer. You can likewise beware of the accommodations and administrations that different financier organizations offer prior to choosing all things considered. These might be administrations, for example, money transformations or giving sufficient data on the stock appraisals. Having listed the upsides and downsides of every one of the business firms, at that point you can choose one that best suits your longing. It is likewise fitting to guarantee that your business organization has an adequate type of money move, particularly for online records. A portion of the organizations will furnish you with Electronic Money Transfer frameworks henceforth improving comfort.

You can get the important endorsement application from your business organization before you can begin purchasing options. You understand that a large portion of the financier firms set cutoff points for their clients; they generally do this so they can keep you from getting wrong dangers that might have been dodged. They additionally do this as they have their own advantages that they are such a lot of ready to secure, particularly on issues to do with the legalities.

Acquaint yourself with the different specialized examination of options; you understand that options are generally present moment. Inability to comprehend the opposition and backing levels, the Fibonacci retracement, the significance of volume, and some fundamental information on the moving midpoints will make it very difficult to experience the interaction easily.

At the point when you get into the genuine trading, it is unseemly to begin trading right away. All things considered, attempt to run some demo accounts and acquaint yourself with them for one month. By doing this, you can attempt to assess your demo returns for certain months and when you locate some degree of consistency in it. You would now be able to assemble the vital certainty and start genuine trading.

At least with these, you will have some premise under which you can base your investigation. Thusly, you will save yourself from enduring high dangers as you know that in the demo account, there are no charges at all that are included.

At the point when you get to trading currently, attempt however much as could reasonably be expected to dodge market prices since they may shift after purchasing or selling the options. This may bring about high yet avoidable misfortunes. All things being equal, set a breaking point request that you find advantageous. For this situation, the exchange might be executed if, by any possibility, the market price arrives at your breaking point or is stunningly better contingent upon whether it's downstream or upstream.

Guarantee that you occasionally reconsider your technique. This guarantees that you take in endlessly from any misstep that you may have submitted during the exchange. For the situation where a portion of your strategies procure great returns, attempt however much as could be expected to use them while as yet attempting to amplify their productivity. Guarantee that you acclimate yourself with new market strategies that may appear to be very productive. You can likewise associate with others that are in the market who have strategies that might be improving in the market than yours. This should construct your certainty, particularly after you endure misfortunes. Having similarly invested individuals in a similar field as you, somewhat, makes you positive about your own self with the end goal that you don't need to beat yourself after you make colossal misfortunes. They assist you with proceeding onward and keep on target while simultaneously minding your technique and making vital changes any place essential. This association additionally gives you a feeling of local area; with this, you can accomplish a specific knowledge into the exchange.

Regardless, it would be astute on the off chance that you remain very centered around your strategies as opposed to differentiating such a huge amount on them. This saves you from wandering off-track as you continued looking for new strategies that may, over the long haul, fizzle.

When you feel that you have acclimated yourself with your present trading strategies, you can attempt to get into some more unpredictable strategies that, over the long haul, procure higher benefits in the event that you will get them. At the point when this is introduced to you, don't be so careless to join the market without attempting a demo represent a few months, this will empower you to improve comprehension of how they run, with this you will have the option to pick whether to proceed with your past strategies or maintain the more perplexing ones. One of these strategies that you can really attempt is the ride system. In this procedure, you purchase the call and the put option at the same time; it shows up as though it is a nonpartisan options technique. Both the call and the put in this offer a similar strike price just as the expiry date. For this situation, you get your benefits for the situation where the prices either go above or underneath the strike price by a sum that is higher or preferably more over that of the premium.

This technique is to some degree very hazardous as it possibly applies when the market is going here and there; in any case, on the off chance that it runs a similar way, just that side will be exercisable.

When you have completely dominated the craft of taking care of even the intricate strategies, don't stop there or lose sight, there is even more to learn. Attempt to boost your benefits however much as could reasonably be expected by acquainting yourself with the measurements which different options dealers use to harvest more benefits. They call it finding out about the Greeks. For this situation, you can utilize the measurements that consider the productivity of benefits. The benefit of benefit alludes to the chance of making in any event a $0.01 benefit on a given exchange. The likelihood of benefit is generally influenced by perspectives as purchasing options, selling options, or the general decrease of stock, or time. This would require a cautious and top to bottom knowledge to understand it completely and use it as your procedure to receive greatest rewards.

CHAPTER 2 UNDERSTANDING OPTIONS

The Call and Put Options

First, we will start with the call option. You can think about this as a deposit for a future purpose. For example, you may be a land developer who wants the right to purchase a lot that is vacant at some point in the future, but you only want to use that right if some zoning laws get put into place that would help you out. The land developer would be able to purchase a call option from the landowner that allows them to purchase the lot at a particular price sometime in the next few years. Now, the landowner does not have to grant this kind of contract for free. The developer will need to add a down payment to lock that right in place; this down payment is known as the premium and is the cost of the options contract. For this one, let us say that the premium on this contract is $6000 that will be paid to the landowners. After two years, the zoning laws have been approved, and the developer will be able to exercise the option to purchase the land for the agreed-upon price. This can be very beneficial to the developer because after the zoning laws went through, the value of the land may double, but the developer will only pay the amount that was originally agreed upon.

The second thing is to use a put option. This is seen as an insurance policy with the stock market. Going back to a land developer, let us say that they own a lot of stocks and they are worried that within the next few years, there will be an issue with a recession in the economy. The developer wants to be sure that if this recession does hit, they will not lose over 10 percent of the value of their stocks. If the stock exchange is trading at 2500, the developer will be able to purchase what is known as a put option, which gives them the right to sell their stocks at 2250 at any point within the next few years. So, if the market ends up crashing down twenty percent in the next six months, they will be able to still sell for 2250, even though the market may have it down to 2000 instead. Even if the market ends up dropping down to zero (which is not likely), the developer will only lose up to ten percent of their portfolio. These examples are used to demonstrate some important points for working with options. First, any time that you purchase an option, you have a right but are not obligated, to do something. You do have the choice to let the expiration go by, and then the option will become worthless. However, if you let the expiration fade, you will lose all of your investment or the option premium. The second thing is that an option is just a contract that will deal with the asset that you want. Because of this, options are considered derivatives. There is another major difference between stock and options. The stock gives any trader a small piece of ownership of a company but in the case of options, they are just contracts that provide the right to buy or sell the stock at a certain price within a specific date. There are always two sides to any option transaction, the buyer, and the seller. This is one important factor that must not be forgotten. Hence, for every call or put that is purchased, there must always be someone selling it.

Option operators must understand the complexity that surrounds them. The knowledge of the operation of the options allows operators to make the right decisions and offers them more options when executing a transaction.

Indicators:

• The price of the guaranteed value

• Expiration

• Implied volatility

• The actual exercise prices

• Dividends

• Interest rates

The "Greeks" provide valuable information on risk management and help rebalance the portfolios to achieve the desired exposure (e.g., delta coverage). Each Greek measures the reaction of the portfolios to small changes in an underlying factor, which allows the individual risks to be examined:

• Theta calculates the sensitivity of the option value over time, a factor known as "temporary wear."

• Vega measures the susceptibility of the option of volatility. Vega measures the value of the option based on the volatility of the underlying asset.

• Therefore, the Greeks are reasonably simple to determine if the Black Scholes model (considered the standard option valuation model) is used and is very useful for intraday and derivatives traders. Delta, Theta, and Vega are useful tools to measure time, price, and volatility.

• For a long period before expiration, the value of the purchase and sale option tends to rise. The opposite situation would occur if, for a short period before expiration, the value of the purchase and sale options is prone to a fall.

• If the volatility increases, so will the value of the purchase and sale options, while if the volatility decreases, the value of the purchase and sale options decreases.

• The price of the guaranteed value causes a different effect on the value of the purchase options than on that of the sale options.

• Usually, as the price of the securities increases, so do the current purchase options that correspond to it, increasing its value while the sale options lose value.

• If the price of the value falls, the opposite happens, and the current purchase options usually experience a drop-in value while the value of the sale options increases.

A bonus of options

It happens when an operator acquires an option contract and pays an initial amount to the seller of the option contract. The option premium will vary depending on when it was calculated and on which market options its acquisition was made.

What is the value of the contract over time?

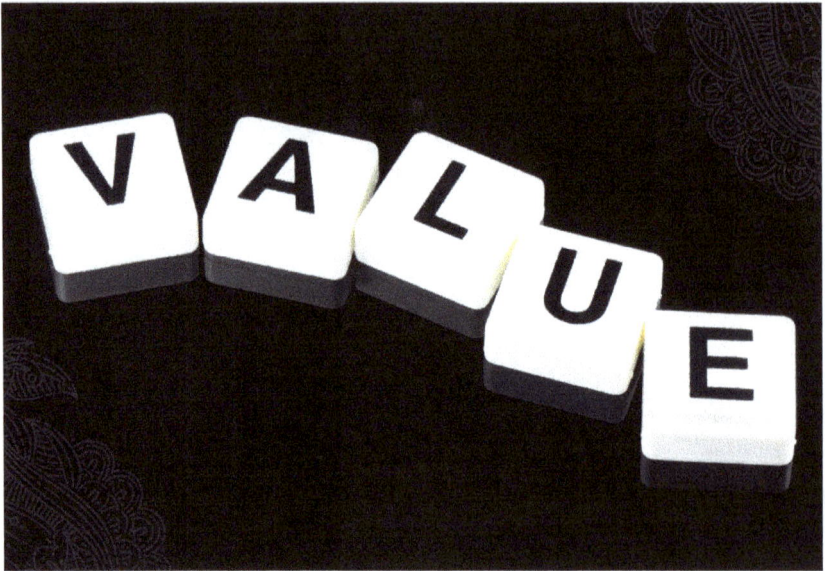

Once an option contract expires, it loses its value. Therefore, it is logical that the longer the validity period, the higher the premium. This is because the deal has additional temporary costs and that more time is available in which the option can be profitable.

What level of volatility does the market have? The premium will be higher if the options market is more volatile as it increases the possibility of obtaining a more significant benefit from the option. The opposite principle applies to the lower volatility that implies a lower premium as the market is considered relatively 'stable'. The volatility of the options market is determined by using different price scales (the long-term, recent, and expected price scales are the required data) to a selection of price volatility models.

The sale and purchase options do not have equivalent values when they reach their mutual ITM, ATM, and OTM exercise price due to the direct and opposite effects caused by their oscillation in irregular distribution curves, which unbalances them.

Exercises —The number of exercises and increments between the exercises are decided based on the change that is applied to the product.

Option valuation models

It is essential to know the differences between historical and implicit volatility when applied for stock market purposes.

Historical volatility calculates the movement rate of the underlying asset in a given time in which the standard annual deviation of price changes is given as a percentage. Historical volatility is the retrospective measurement at the date of calculation of the information available on the degree of instability of the underlying asset in a given number of trading days (modifiable period) and during a selected period.

The implied volatility is the future approximation of the stock exchange volume of the underlying asset that measures the expected variation in the standard daily deviation of the asset between the date on which it is calculated and the maturity of the option. When analyzing the value of an option, implied volatility is one of the critical factors that an operator has to consider. To calculate implied volatility, an option valuation model is used, taking into account the cost of the option premium.

There are three types of theoretical valuation models that intraday traders use most frequently as an aid to assess implied volatility. These models are the Black-Scholes, the Bjerksund-Stensland, and the Binomial. With them, the calculation is done using algorithms, usually buy and sell options are used at-the-money or nearest-the-money.

The Black-Scholes model is the most used with European options (these options may only be executed on the day of expiration).

The Bjerksund – Stensland model is very efficient if applied to US options that can be executed at any time between the acquisition of the contract and its expiration.

The Binomial model is appropriately applied to American, European, and Bermuda options. Bermudas are a midpoint between European and American companies and can be executed only on certain days of the contract or on the expiration date.

Types of options:

There are two main kinds of options:

1. Selling options: a given option is an option contract wherein the owner can but is not required to sell a specified amount of the underlying security at a given price within a certain period. This is the opposite of a purchase option. It gives the holder the right to purchase shares.

A sale option becomes more valuable as the price of the underlying share depreciates relative to the exercise price. On the contrary, a sale option loses its value as the underlying share appreciates and its maturity approaches.

The value of a sale option decreases with time since the chances of the stock falling below the specified strike price are less and less with time.

2. The purchase options: A call option is an agreement that gives the investor the right to buy stocks, bonds, commodities, or other instruments at a specified price within a specified period, but not the obligation.

The purchase option gives you the right to purchase an asset. When the underlying asset increases in price, you get benefits with a buy option. For example, if your share is priced at $50 and you buy your purchase option at $50, then you have the right to buy that share at $50, regardless of its price, as long as the time has not failed. Even if the stock goes up to $ 100, you still have the right to buy that stock for $ 50.

The underlying asset

Traditionally, most options have been based on shares of publicly traded companies. However, options based on other underlying investments are increasingly common. This includes options based on stock indices, traded funds (ETF), REIT (real estate investment funds), foreign exchange, and raw materials such as agricultural or industrial products. When it comes to stock option contracts, it is essential to keep in mind that they are based on 100 shares of the underlying value.

CHAPTER 3 UNDERSTANDING OPTIONS CONTRACTS

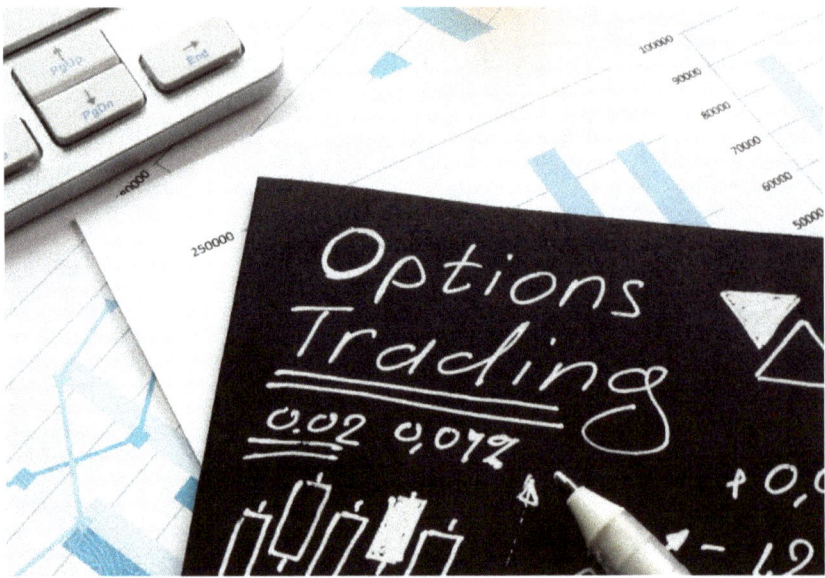

Different Types of Options Trading

An option is a deal between two parties for the purchase or selling of an asset at a fixed amount before a fixed date. Before looking at the different types of options available, let us quickly look at the details that the option contract will contain.

The first thing that the option contract will decide is if the holder of the option has the right to buy (call option) or the right to sell (put option). Another essential piece of information is the quantity and value of the underlying asset. By this, we mean the number and form of shares to be purchased or sold. The third significant piece of information to be stated in the contract is the strike price (i.e., the investor will pay for the asset when the option is exercised). The fourth element to be stated in the contract will be the expiry date of the option (i.e., the last day on which the option may be exercised). The terms of the settlement will be the fifth thing to be included in the contract. This indicates that the seller will deliver the actual asset or an equal sum of cash. Ultimately, the last piece of detail contained in the option contract is the amount paid by the holder to the seller of the right.

Taking a look at the various types of options that are available:

1. Exchange - traded option or listed options – these are a form of exchange-traded derivatives. Exchange-exchanged securities are exchanged

through specialist derivative markets. Those are markets where individuals are trading structured contracts that have been formulated by an exchange. A clearinghouse resolves such agreements. As the deals are structured, it is easier to provide reliable pricing models for these products. Such options include Stock-Options based on the stock of a firm.

2. Consumer - Options for consumer goods. These are goods for which there is global demand and which are similar in that it does not matter who makes them. Those are essential resources and agricultural products, such as oil, sugar, and cotton.

3. Bonds – Bonds are debt insurance, that is a deal to repay borrowed money with interest at fixed intervals. The bond choice is a choice to purchase or sell a bond at a specific price on or before the expiry date. In Europe, the language of Bond Options varies from that of the United States. In Europe, a bond contract is an option to buy or sell a bond for a fixed price at a specific date in the future. In the US, the choice of a relationship is to buy or sell a

relationship on or before a particular time for a fixed price in the future.

4. Stock market index - These options are related to the price of the indices, either broad-based indices such as S&P500 or narrow-based index, which are indices confined to a specific industry. This choice offers the right to exchange a specified stock index at a given price by the stated expiry date.

5. Future Contracts - In futures contracts, the strike price (price paid when an option is exercised) is the stated futures price at which the future is exchanged if the option is used.

CBBC is a derivative, typically issued by third parties, usually investment banks (never stock exchanges or asset owners) that gives investors leveraged investment in underlying assets.

6. Over-the-counter or Dealer Options - These are traded between two private parties and are not included in an auction. The terms of the contract of the OTC are unlimited and can be written to match the needs of the company in question. The different

types of OTCs are interest rates, cross-currency, and swaps (Stations).

Stations give the owner the right, not the duty, to join the underlying exchange.

7. Other forms of option: employee stock, given to workers as reimbursement for hard work, real estate, often used to build up vast parcels of land, and prepayment, used in mortgage loans.

Various types of choices include European, American, Bermudan, Firewall, Exotic, and Vanilla options (the vanilla option being any alternative that is not exotic).

8. American and European options

European options can only be utilized on their expiry date, while American options can be used on or before that date. American options take effect on the third Saturday of each month and are closed for trading on the previous Friday. In contrast, European options expire on the third Friday of each month and are closed for trading the last Thursday.

In both styles, the pay-off is measured as the maximum of the strike amount minus the spot amount or zero, for a call The peak of the spot price minus the strike price or zero, for a call If the American and European options are otherwise similar (with the same strike price, etc.), the American would be worth at least as much as the European option. If it finds out it is worth more, the difference in value may in use to determine whether or not it should be practiced before the expiry date.

Options contracts exchanged on exchanges are primarily American, while options traded over the counter are predominantly European.

9. Bermudan options The Bermudan option may be exercised on different dates on or before the expiry date. It is halfway between European (allowing exercise at one time) and American (allowing practice at any time) options. Most of the exotic interest rate plans are Bermudan type options.

10. Barrier Options Barrier Options may only be exercised once the price of the underlying asset has

reached a certain point or barrier. Barriers are always cheaper than non-barriers and have been designed to encourage investors to hedge options without having to pay too high a premium.

The two forms of barrier options are 'in' and 'out' options – 'in' options start their lives worthless and become active when the barrier is reached, while 'out' options start their lives vigorously and become ineffective once the barrier is breached. Both types may be divided into two separate categories-up-and-out or down-and-out, or up-and-down and down-and-in.

- Up-and-Out: the spot value starts below the barrier and has to rise for the option to end

- Down-and-out: the spot value starts above the barrier level and has to decline for the option to end

- Up-and-in: the spot price starts below the boundary rate and has to increase for the option to be activated

- Down-and-in: the spot price begins above the barrier level and has to fall.

CHAPTER 4   THE   OPTIONS MARKET

A vital aspect of options trading is the platform that one uses to trade. This is because options trading requires monitoring and requires a continuous analysis of trends. Performance is also monitored, and since the trade is impacted upon by a complex of factors, one has to choose a suitable platform for trading.

Types of Trading Platforms

There are various platforms in options trading that one could consider. There is web-based trading that utilizes the power of the search engines. This platform has many operators since the building of websites in the modern age is easy. This platform is responsible for the growth in the popularity of options trading. People can trade from anyone, open brokerage accounts, make deposits, and participate in the buying and selling of assets in the comfort of their homes.

With the presence of a lot of technological gadgets such as smartphones, tablets, and computers, web-based trading has been easy and possible. Websites can be built with additional resources for learning and tools that can be an advantage for both novice and seasoned traders.

The web is also a good platform when it comes to filtering opportunities and options based on suitability and preference in view of the various abilities of users. They can be designed to be customizable even when the options markets are standardized.

Usually, websites are good as they offer various tools that aid beginners to edge into trading options. ASX, for example, offers a variety of web-based resources that guide people in their efforts to understand trading. This includes online chats that have instant feedback as a team is dedicated to the work site for correspondence purposes. The aim of this is to offer motivation and impetus to go on with the discovery of the markets trends until one becomes a seasoned trader.

Friendliness is also in terms of the efforts that are made to create peer assistance. This is through creating groups of traders that influence each other and can learn from the vast experiences in the trading of the options. This can be a positive influence on the journey to gaining competence and help support an environment where people can relate and interact as they pursue their various financial goals.

It is important to consider the fact that some of the platforms of trading offer important tools that can be helpful in deciding on options. The tools are those that help in monitoring markets and simplify the technical analysis process for the trader. This can help one to sharpen their trading strategy to align well with the ultimate goal of trading. This depends on whether the goal of trading is to earn money in terms of profit or hedge oneself against losses on the underlying asset.

Tools to Learn

Upon mastering the various basics of trading and making the initial moves to start trading, one has to use various tools that help to indicate the advancers and decliners on the market. Greeks are some kind of metrics that those involved in options trading capitalize to ensure maximization of returns. These "Greeks" include the delta matrix that measures the correlation between price movements of the underlying asset relative to the price of the option

The gamma is another tool that can help to predict market trends in order to do good timing for decisions on exercising rights in options. Gamma is an indicator of the rate of delta variations for the option price as compared to the asset price. This goes hand in hand with the time-decay tool that indicators the value movement, either upwards or downwards, in the period of life options. This helps to signal which options to avoid given the remaining time of the life span and the value implications thereon.

There is also the aspect of the volatility of the asset underlying a particular option trade. Some of the assets or stocks do not have inherent volatility to appreciate in value due to their nature. Assets that have high market volatility usually gain a lot on the market, and hence, the value behaves better to favor the call option trade. Products with ugh volatility and high inherent value are not suitable for the put option trade since they will occasion a loss. It is therefore important to use correct tools that aid in the analysis if the technical mechanics of the options trading business.

Tools are not just concrete things that can be manipulated. Some tools, especially in trading, are conceptual in nature. This is because they are the ones by which one can trade and aid in decision making. They sample out market forces and help in mapping out market trends for the benefit of the trader. To perceive tools as only concrete in nature is a misconception of the whole options trading venture.

Professional level platforms

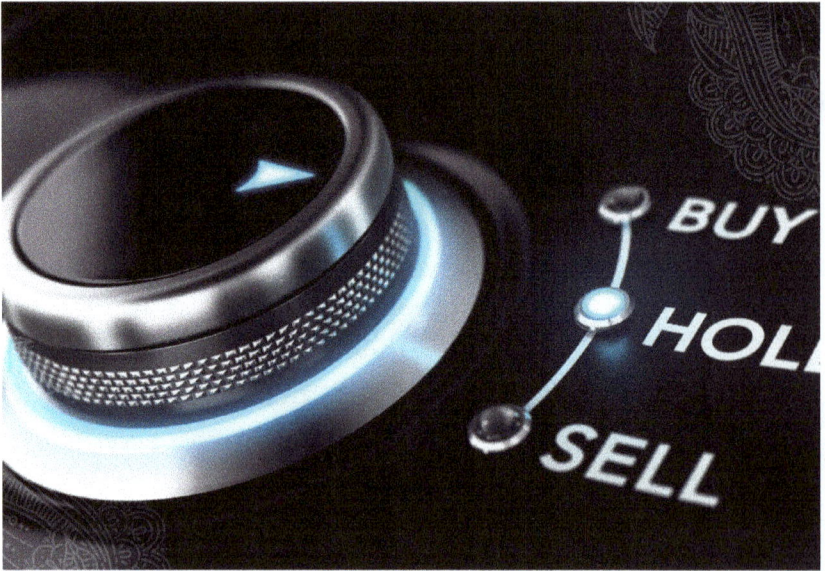

There is a level in trading where one attains sophistication and attains the intuition to thrive in options trading regardless of the ways market forces seem to behave. At this level, someone needs tools that can help them edge into the horizon of complexity in trading. The platforms for this professional level exist, and they have to offer tools that are an edge above the basic level. These tools have to offer strategies of competing to control the stocks and rise above the market forces. At this level, one becomes daring, and the possibilities that the platform offers should only be dared by those who have mastered trading and are sure of beating odds as they speculate about squeezing out value form trades that otherwise be perceived as highly risky.

The platform should be full of idea probing resources that lead one to gain the courage to trade more and more. Web-based platforms of this level include the think or swim platform that is categorically for seasoned traders. This is the reason why one has to know the platform to trade on based on their level of experience in options trading. Some platforms are too complicated for the starters. The tools are even out of the capacity of a beginner to comprehend the trades appear to have higher risks that may wipe away hard-earned fortunes.

Mobile Trading

Some platforms have taken advantage of the handiness of the mobile era. These entail the smartphone lifestyle and the flashier iPod, iPad, and tablet culture. This is when trading is being placed in the palms of traders to hold and run away with it. This platform usually targets traders that want to capitalize on device optimization. This is the reason why trades have classes. Some of the options could be device targeted as they can only be taken advantage of when one using the suitable device for trading, provided the relevant support tools that the device offers.

Mobile trading also comes in order to keep people abreast. This is because opportunities sometimes appear and disappear on people because they are not using a device that enables them to be precise and timely in decision making and action.

With mobile trading, apps have been developed, some with notification capability. One can customize the apps to ensure that no opportunity comes that is not taken advantage of. Opportunities' in trading have to be seized and relying on a platform that is less handy and far means that opportunities of trading are lost.

What Are We Looking for in Platforms and Tools?

First is the opportunity to learn. There is no worse platform of trading than that which targets only to admit traders who do not understand what they are getting into. The education that a platform has to offer should be free as trading is itself risky enough to prohibit any extra expenses in the process. Platform operators should understand that any interested person who visits their platform is a potential subscriber, and they should freely offer support to educate them for the purpose of acquisition of requisite knowledge on options trading.

Some of the platforms have gone as opening structures units for education on options trading. These courses are taken online, and coaching is done through the provision of a stream of webinars transmitted live or uploading recorded ones. This is for platforms that appreciate that trading is an informed gamble that requires one to know enough. They even test the proficiency of understanding trading concepts and mechanics for the purpose of ensuring that any people who trade on the platform are doing what they understand to build the platform ratings.

It is also vital for a starter to set standards that the broker's customer service should pass. In trading, brokers should work enough to earn the commission that they charge on the options that subscribers trade on buy. This is because some brokers are obscure and may not involve the options trader who is buying options in decisions that directly impact on his capital. One, therefore, faces a lot of anxiety if the broker is not responsive and transparent on the particular mechanics that influence trade.

Excellent broker services try to suit customer needs. They ask options traders subscribed to their platform what their preferred means of reaching is. Whether a live chat or phone call suits the customer or not. They also dedicate a desk for trading communications and queries and has the discipline to listen to customers and their issues with patience.

Software Trading Platforms

These are more complex than web-based ones. This is because they are run on the trader's computer, and the trader is required to understand what the software does and interpret it. Even when the brokerage can offer assistance, software-based platforms require the trader to have enough technical know how to read charts, graphs, and understand patterns that represent various components of options trading.

For beginners, a complex platform has to be avoided by all means. This is because one is bound to engage in aspects of trading that they do not have an understanding of. A trading platform simply has to be simple and clear. The interface should not be too busy as to scare away those traders who are not accustomed. This is the reason why operators usually separate the platforms that as designed for basic use, which is suitable for novices, and advanced trading for the seasoned ones.

Then a broker has to offer a tutorial that guides the user on how to navigate their platform. Everything has to be explained, even those that one would deem to be obvious. Screenshots can even be available in order to be categorical and emphatic. This ensures that a broker has offered all possible assists for the trader to benefit from the offers and products on the platform successfully.

Cost Implication

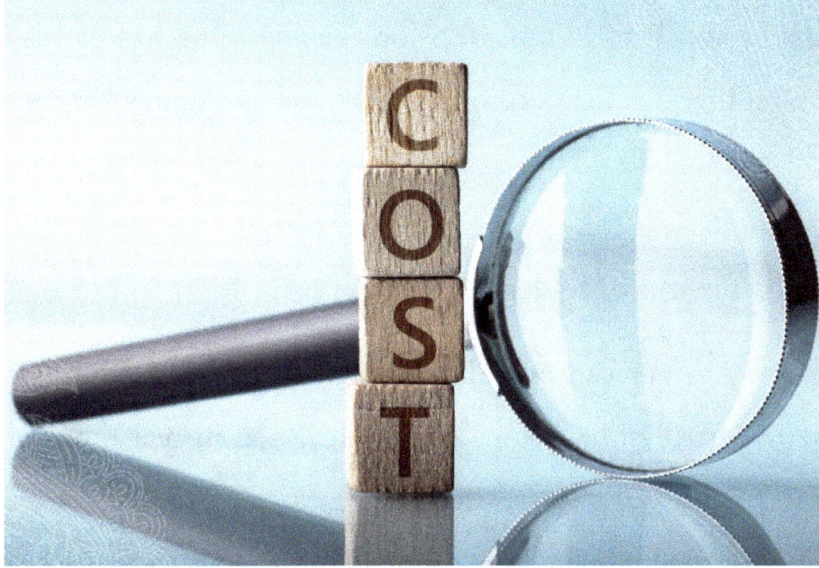

It is important for the trader to know that some brokers may have charges attached to some of the services, resources, and tools that they provide on their platform. These have to be assessed in terms of their worth and whether the costs are necessary. Making some tolls premium may be an indicator of quality but not always. This is particularly the case when other platforms provide similar services toll-free.

Screening tools are particularly the ones that are bound to attract charges because they have abilities to analyze and assess market trends. They can do the thinking for the trader and help him in decision making. One has to read about the specifications of the tools and ascertain what they or cannot do. This is in order to know if they are customizable for the purpose of serving the needs and conveniences of traders.

Some charges can even be attached to the quotes update feed. Usually, the quotes can be accessed in real time for those who want to see them in real time. The quotes are important in influencing idea generation and sometimes can tip people of opportunities in the market. There is usually a delay for those who access the quotes updates for free.

CHAPTER 5   THE GREEKS

These elements are called Greeks since they are routinely associated with Greek pictures/images. Each danger variable is an outcome of an imperfect speculation or relationship of the option with another fundamental variable.

Delta

Delta (Δ) implies the pace of progress between the option's price and a $1 change in the basic resource's price. By the day's end, the price affectability of the option relative with the hidden. For example, expect a monetary expert is long a call option with a delta of 0.50. Along these lines, if the hidden stock additions by $1, the option's price would theoretically increase by 50 pennies.

For options brokers, delta moreover means the support extent for making a delta-unprejudiced position. Net delta for a plan of options can in like manner be used to get the portfolio's fence extent.

Theta

Theta (Θ) connotes the pace of progress between the time and option price, or time affectability - now and again known as an option's time decay. Theta shows the aggregate an option's price would lessen as the time to termination reduces, all else same. For example, acknowledge a monetary expert is long an option with a theta of - 0.50.

The option's price would decrease by 50 pennies reliably that passes, all else being same. In the event that three trading days' pass, the option's worth would speculatively lessen by $1.50.

Theta increases when options are at-the-money, and lessens when options are in-and out-of-the-money. Options nearer to end in like manner have animating time decay. Long puts and long calls will for the most part have negative Theta; short puts and short calls will have positive Theta. Conversely, an instrument whose value isn't broken down by time, for instance, a stock, would have zero Theta.

Gamma

Gamma (Γ) means the pace of progress between the fundamental resource's price and an option's delta. This is called second-request price affectability.

Gamma shows the entirety the delta would change given a $1 move in the fundamental security. For instance, what about we expect a monetary trained professional or financial specialist is long one call option on theoretical stock XYZ.

Vega

Vega (V) implies the speed of progress between the fundamental resource's inferred instability and an option's value. This is the option's affectability to unpredictability. Vega shows the amount of an option's price changes given a 1 rate change in suggested instability.

Since extended unpredictability infers that the fundamental instrument will undoubtedly experience ludicrous values, a rising in instability will correspondingly construct the value of an option. Then again, a decrease in unpredictability will unfavorably impact the value of the option. Vega is at its generally outrageous for at-the-money options that have longer times until end.

Minor Greeks

These are second-or third-subsidiaries of the evaluating model and influence things, for example, the adjustment in delta with an adjustment in instability, and so forth They are continuously used in options trading philosophies as PC programming can quickly measure and record for these perplexing and sometimes slippery danger factors.

Benefits and Risk from Buying Call Options

The call options let the holder buy a hidden security at the communicated strike price by the termination date called the expiry. The holder doesn't resolve to buy the resource in the event that they would not really like to purchase the resource. The danger to the call option buyer is confined to the exceptional paid. Changes in the hidden stock don't influence.

Benefits and Risk from Selling Call Options

Selling call options is known as creating an arrangement. The author gets the top notch expense. Toward the day's end, an option buyer will pay the premium to the merchant—or author—of an option. The most outrageous benefit is the superior gotten when selling the option. A financial specialist who sells a call option is bearish and acknowledges the basic stock's price will fall or remain respectably close to the option's strike price during the existence of the option.

In the event that the transcendent piece of the pie price is at or under the strike price by expiry, the option lapses uselessly for the call buyer. The option trader pockets the premium as their benefit.

Benefits and Risks from Buying Put Options

Put options are investments where the buyer accepts the fundamental stock's market price will fall underneath the strike price prior to the lapse date of the option. The holder can offer offers without the obligation to sell at the communicated strike per-share price by the expressed date.

Since buyers of put options need the stock price to reduce, the put option is beneficial when the fundamental stock's price is underneath the strike price. In the event that the overarching market price isn't actually the strike price at expiry, the speculator can rehearse the put. Their benefit on this exchange is the strike price less the current market price, notwithstanding costs—the premium and any business commission to present the orders. The result would be expanded by the quantity of option contracts purchased, by then increased by 100—expecting every understanding/contract addresses 100 offers.

Benefits and Risks from Selling Put Options

Selling put options is generally called creating an understanding or an agreement. A put option creator acknowledges the essential stock's expense will stay the proportionate or expansion over the existence of the option—making them

bullish on the offers.

Here, the option buyer has the advantage to make the dealer, buy parts of the hidden resource at the strike price on expiry.

On the off chance that the hidden stock's price closes over the strike price by the termination date, the put option slips by uselessly. The essayist's most prominent benefit is the premium.

On the off chance that the stock market's value drops underneath the option strike price, the put option author is resolved to buy portions of the fundamental stock at the strike price. All things considered, the put option will be rehearsed by the option buyer.

The buyer will sell their proposals at the strike price since it is higher than the stock market's value.

The danger for the put option essayist happens when the market's price falls under the strike price. As of now, at termination, the vendor is constrained to purchase shares at the strike price. Dependent upon how much the offers have recognized, the put author's misfortune can be colossal.

The put author—the shipper—can either hang on the offers and expectation the stock price rises above the price tag or sell the offers and accept the misfortune. Regardless, any misfortune is counterbalanced reasonably by the top notch got.

Sometimes a monetary expert will make put options at a strike price that is the spot they see the offers being a nice value and would buy at that price. Exactly when the price falls, and the option buyer rehearses their option, they get the stock at the price they need, with the extra bit of leeway of getting the option premium.

Geniuses

A call option buyer has the advantage to buy resources at a price that is lesser than the market when the stock's price is expanding.

The put option buyer can benefit by selling the stock at the strike price when the market price is underneath the strike price.

Option shippers get a superior vibe from the buyer for forming an option.

Cons

In a falling business sector, the put option vendor may be constrained to buy the resource at the higher strike price than they would consistently pay on the lookout.

The call option creator faces interminable danger if the stock's price rises by and large and they are constrained to buy shares at an excessive cost.

Option buyers should pay a straightforward premium to the creators of the option.

True Example of an Option

Expect that Microsoft shares are trading at $108 per offer and you acknowledge that they are going to increase in value. You decide to buy a call option to benefit by a development in the stock's price.

You get one call option with a strike price of $115 for one month later for 37 pennies for each contact. Your total money cost is $37 for the circumstance, notwithstanding commissions and charges (0.37 x 100 = $37).

The benefit on the option position would be 170.3%

since you paid 37 pennies and procured $1—that is much higher than the 7.4%

extension in the fundamental stock price from $108 to $116 at the hour of expiry.

On the off chance that the stock tumbled to $100, your option would terminate uselessly, and you would be out $37 premium. The potential gain is that you didn't buy 100

shares at $108, which would have achieved a $8 per share, or $800, full scale misfortune. As ought to be self-evident, options can restrict your disadvantage hazard. In a manner of speaking, the benefit in dollar terms would be a net of 63 pennies or $63 since one option contract connotes 100 offers ($1 - 0.37 x 100 = $63).

If the stock tumbled to $100, your option would slip by pointlessly, and you would be out $37 premium. The potential gain is that you didn't acknowledge 100 proposals at $108, which would have achieved a $8 per share, or $800, complete misfortune. As ought to be self-evident, options can help limit your disadvantage peril.

Options Spreads

Options spreads are methods that use distinctive blends of buying and selling different options for an ideal danger bring profile back. Spreads are created using vanilla options, and can abuse various circumstances, for instance, high-or low-unpredictability conditions, up-or down-moves, or anything in the center.

Spread frameworks, can be depicted by their outcome or view of their benefit misfortune profile, for instance, bull call spreads or iron condors.

CHAPTER 6   ADVANTAGES AND RISKS

Advantages of Trading Options

There are several advantages to trading options and they include:

• The initial investment is lower than with trading stocks. This means that the options trader can benefit from playing in the same financial market as a stocks trader without paying as much upfront. This is called hedging.

• The options trader is not required to own the asset to benefit from its value. This means that the trader does not incur the cost associated with the asset. Costs can include transportation and storage fees if applicable.

• There is no obligation to follow through with the transaction. Whether the trader is exercising a call or put option, at the end of the day, the loss is limited because the trader is only obligated to pay for the contract and nothing more. Only if the trader feels it worth it does he or she take action to move forward with exercising the contract.

• The options trader has many choices. Trading options gives the trader great flexibility. Traders can choose to:

o   Sell the options to another investor in the case of in the money situations.

o   Exercise the contract and buy the asset.

o   Exercise the option and sell all or part of the asset.

o   In the case of out of the money situations, sell the options to another investor before the expiration date arrives.

• The strike price freezes the price. This allows the options trader the ability to buy or sell the asset on or before the expiration date without the worry of fluctuating prices.

• Options can protect an asset from depreciating market prices. This is a long-term strategy that can protect assets from drops in the market prices. Exercising a call allows the trader to buy the asset at a lower price.

• The trader can earn passive income from assets that he or she already owns. You can sell call options on your own assets to earn income through traders paying you premiums.

There are many advantages to trading using options, but you don't get all those benefits without taking on-board some element of risk. A notable risk that you have to accept is that options have a limited lifespan as they are limited by expiry date. Now there are clear strategies that you must have in place when handling this risk such as having an exit strategy. For example, your choices are, trade the option during the timespan of the option, expire the option on or before the expiry date or simply let the option expire.

However, there can be a big problem with just leaving options to expire. For example, if the option is in-the-money at expiration, your broker may well automatically exercise/assign the option. The problem here is that by exercising the valuable option they have effectively converted a low-cost option position into a high-cost stock position, which you may not want or be able to afford. Consequently, you need to carefully monitor your options and check for notifications from the broker platform regarding any in-the-money option positions, which are nearing the expiration date. You need to do this in anticipation of this likely change in your margin requirement. Alternatively, you want to make sure you have sufficient time to trade the option or make other adjustments such as rolling over a trade in order to avoid buying the stock.

Risk of Leverage

Another significant risk to be aware of is that of leverage. Because Options don't cost much as stock as they are simply a contract, this means that they experience disproportionately larger percentage price gains in reaction to the far more expensive underlying stock's very small price movements. The huge benefit of this is that it results in large percentage gains when the underlying stock moves in the anticipated direction by even a small amount. The downside though is that it also results in a 100% wipe-out of the investment if the stock moves by even the smallest amount in the wrong direction. This is not necessarily an issue with beginners or at least it shouldn't be as the risk manifests itself mainly through trading too large a position size. However, you need to be aware that as beneficial as leverage clearly is, it can also be a double edge sword, so be aware that leverage is a risk that needs to be addressed. One simple way to nullify or minimize this level of risk is to keep your position size small.

Trading rules, you should know

Whenever you begin trading a new market, you'll need to become acquainted very quickly with the trading rules. Usually, your broker or their trading platform will prevent you from going wrong, but you shouldn't need to rely on them to keep you right. We provide a short list of common basic rules for trading Options that will hopefully help you through your initial trading executions and throughout your trading career:

• Contract pricing: In general Options trade in increments of $0.01, $0.05, and $0.10.

• Option premium: The price of the premium that you pay for an option is obtained by multiplying the option price offered by the multiplier. When trading in stocks the multiplier value is usually based upon 100 shares of the underlying stock. Therefore, when you purchase one option that is quoted at $2.80, you are actually going to have to pay $2,80 x 100 = $280 for the option, plus any broker commission.

• Market conditions: There are different market conditions that impact both the stock and options markets. These include the following:

• Trading halts for security or entire market: If you find yourself holding an option for a halted stock, then any options based on the stock will also be halted. This does not affect your rights or prevent you from exercising your contract rights. However, be aware that when this occurs before expiration it may be difficult to trade the options but will not prevent you from exercising the option on or before the expiry date.

• Fast trading conditions: In fast-moving markets stock prices can change rapidly and you are likely to see quotes changing quickly. As a result, when you are placing an order you might find that there are significant delays. This can simply be because your bid is not falling out with the bid-ask spread so is being ignored. Therefore, you need to check and if necessary, to edit your order to make it more acceptable. Also, in fast moving market conditions make sure to use limit orders that are price focused rather than market orders as you may end up paying more than you wanted.

Good risk management enables the trader to ensure his survival and therefore to retain his most valuable work tool, namely his capital. A ruined trader no longer can exercise his activity. In addition, risk management allows it to focus primarily on the best opportunities. Indeed, there are multiple opportunities in the markets, but the trader must first select those that offer the lowest risk for a high potential of gain.

A trader who manages his risk correctly controls the probabilities. Indeed, the biggest danger in trading is to think you have found the magic formula because it is easy to be intoxicated by success and to believe yourself infallible. If you follow Sun Tzu, a person who thinks he is infallible becomes extremely vulnerable. Therefore, the trader must manage his risk even more strictly after a series of winnings. Unfortunately, this situation often corresponds to a euphoric state of the trader who begins to have disproportionate confidence in his "instinct" and ends up making dramatic mistakes.

The Art of Achieving One's Goals Without Taking Risks

Contrary to a widespread belief, the best traders take a very little risk. They put risk management at the top of their trading plan. Performance is only the result of strict monitoring of the plan. When the title evolves against its original scenario, the trader must seek to get out of his position as soon as possible. He can, of course, wait for a rebound to come out with a lesser loss, but he must never drag on and go into hope mode.

Linda Bradford Marschke explains the importance of testing the markets: "In trading, part of the process involves testing the markets. If the timing of your entry is good enough, you will not lose much even when you are wrong."

In trading, you must manage your risk and the profits will come naturally, the art of lasting is it not the key to success? The trader must identify situations where the risk is low (close stop) and the potential for high gain. He will have to avoid situations where the risk is too high even if the

78

potential is interesting and wait only for the best opportunities.

One must always think about the consequences of one's actions. The ruin is the financial death of the trader. Indeed, it is difficult in this case to go back and rebuild its capital. The trader must above all aim for survival even when he is at the top of his game. Indeed, it is often at this moment that it is the most fragile.

Sometimes Escape Is the Best Alternative

According to Paul Tudor Jones, "we must always favor defense to attack". If we have a losing position that places us in an uncomfortable situation, there is a simple rule: to get out of his position at any cost in order to regain his senses and wait for a new interesting entry point. It is always possible to come back, and a trader must convince himself that there is nothing better than a fresh start.

Bruce Kovner evokes the importance he gives to his stops, (a level that invalidates our scenario and must trigger an exit from our position): "Every time I open a position, I have a predetermined stop. This is the only way for me to sleep. I know where I'm going before, I get home. I always place my stop over a technical barrier. A technical barrier is a level that the market should not touch if our scenario is good. I organized my life so that my stops are followed religiously."

During doubtful phases, the trader should stay out of the markets. It is useless to position ourselves if the probabilities are not favorable to us. You do not have to be in the market all the time. This exhibition is vain and useless. The leak can be beneficial in trading. It is even, for P. Fayyad, "the stratagem of the stratagems". Indeed, when a conflict cannot find a favorable outcome, the best choice is the leak because it means that the trader preserves his capital for better times, which will not fail to occur.

To summarize, the trader will have to survive on the markets first and foremost. Profits are only the natural result of the application of his "survival" plan.

CONCLUSION

Thank you for making it to the end. Whatever your reasons for trading options, you might have questions about how to do it effectively. That's why we have this Options Trading Crash Course.

The primary purpose of trading options is to make money by essentially buying an option contract so that you can sell it before the expiration date. There are two types of options contracts: call and put. You can also buy a combination of calls and puts, known as a synthetic option. These contracts are bought for two reasons: to gain exposure to an asset, and to profit from a shift in the underlying asset's value as time passes.

Options have grown in popularity because they offer investors with potential high profits without investment risk. However, like any investment, there are risks associated with options. When you buy an option, you are giving up an opportunity to make money, but if you don't buy an option at all, then you're taking on nothing but risk.

If volatility increases or decreases, then the price of an underlying asset could move in either direction very differently than anticipated.

There are tremendous benefits to trading options. We understand the challenges investors face when trading options. That is why we wrote this book.

Options Trading can be very profitable if you know what you are doing.

Trading options is a very simple process. If you want to buy it, then look for a stock that is about to go up and buy it with the option in order to profit sometime in the future. If the stock goes up the option gives you more profit over time so the total profit would be higher than if you had only bought the stock.

On the other hand, if you want to sell the option, then look for a stock that is about to go down and sell it with the option in order to profit sometime in the future. If the stock goes down, then your gain will be larger than if you had only sold the stock without this option.

If you're new to options trading or are unsure about how to best invest your money, we're here to assist. This book is always available to answer any preliminary questions you may have.

If, on the other hand, you want to have some more information and dive deeper into the world of options trading to discover the winning strategies, the most profitable assets, to learn day trading, swing trading and everything else, we invite you to discover the other manuals in the series:

OPTIONS TRADING CRASH COURSE: INVESTING FOR BEGINNERS *Learn how to operate in the market in the best way even if you are just a beginner*

OPTIONS TRADING CRASH COURSE: SWING TRADING, DAY TRADING AND BEST STRATEGIES *The best strategies to operate in the market in the most profitable way*

OPTIONS TRADING CRASH COURSE: ADVANCED OPTIONS TRADING TOOLS *A simple* *but effective guide to operate in the market in a smart and conscious way*